Created to Dream

The 6 Phases God Uses to Grow Your Faith

BIBLE STUDY GUIDE | SIX SESSIONS

RICK WARREN

HarperChristian Resources

Created to Dream Bible Study Guide
Original edition © 2010 by Rick Warren
Updated edition © 2023 by Rick Warren

The *Created to Dream* Bible Study is an updated and expanded version of the previously published *Everything Is Possible with God.*

Requests for information should be addressed to:
HarperChristian Resources, 3900 Sparks Dr. SE, Grand Rapids, Michigan 49546

ISBN: 978-0-310-16287-2 (softcover)
ISBN: 978-0-310-16288-9 (e-book)

23 24 25 26 27 LBC 5 4 3 2 1

Contents

A Note from
Rick Warren

What does God think of you? What is his opinion of you? When God thinks of you, he doesn't shake his head about your past. He dreams about your future. He doesn't say to himself, "Well, I guess I made a mistake when I made this one." He says, "Wow, have I got plans for your life!"

God thinks about you all the time. And his thoughts are good thoughts, filled with hope and purpose. The Bible says, *"How precious are your thoughts about me, O God. They cannot be numbered! I can't even count them; they outnumber the grains of sand!"* (Psalm 139:17–18 NLT).

Are you getting the message? God isn't mad at you. He's mad about you. Your picture is taped to his refrigerator. You are the constant object of his attention. He created you to love you—and he created you to dream.

You might be thinking, *Surely you can't be talking about me. I doubt that God ever thinks about me, or if he does, I'm sure he's disappointed. He can't possibly have a dream for my life.*

Whoever told you that was not telling the truth. It is never too late to follow God's dream, because his plan takes into account all the mistakes you have made. There is nothing about you that is a surprise to God. He has seen every moment of your life—every failure, every sin, every heartache—and he invites you even now to pursue his plan for you.

Friend, our God is a God of miracles. He has a plan and a purpose for your life, and he always keeps his promises. Do you believe that everything is possible with God? Jesus said, *"According to your faith let it be done to you"* (Matthew 9:29 NIV). I pray this study will strengthen your faith and prepare you to go after the amazing dream God has for you.

— RICK WARREN

Understanding Your
Study Guide

Here is a brief explanation of the features of this study guide:

Looking Ahead/Catching Up: You will open each meeting by briefly discussing a question that will help focus everyone's attention on the subject of the lesson.

Key Verse: Each session you will find a key Bible verse for your group to read together. If someone in the group has a different translation, ask them to read it aloud so the group can get a bigger picture of the meaning of the passage.

Video Lesson: There is a video lesson for the group to watch together each week. Fill in the blanks in the session outline as you watch the video, and be sure to refer back to these outlines during your discussion time.

Living on Purpose: Each video segment is complemented by four application questions for group discussion. There is no reason to rush through the answers. Give everyone ample opportunity to share their thoughts. If you don't get through all the discussion questions, that's okay.

Prayer Direction: At the end of each session, you will find suggestions for your group prayer time. Praying together is one of the greatest privileges of small group life. Please don't take it for granted.

Putting It into Practice: This is where the rubber meets the road. We don't want to be just hearers of the Word. We also need to be doers of the Word (see James 1:22).

These assignments are application exercises that will help your group discuss ways to put into practice the truths they are learning.

Between the Sessions: To encourage participants to engage with Pastor Rick's message throughout the week, a personal study is provided after each session. This non-video-based section of the study guide includes additional reading and reflection questions, divided into three days.

A Tip for the Host

The study guide material is meant to be your servant, not your master. The point is not to race through the sessions; the point is to take time to let God work in your lives. Nor is it necessary to "go around the circle" before you move on to the next question. Give people the freedom to speak, but don't insist on it. Your group will enjoy deeper, more open sharing and discussion if people don't feel pressured to speak up.

How *Faith* and *Dreaming* Are Connected

Looking Ahead

Take a few minutes to introduce yourselves to your group and to review the Group Guidelines on page 91. Then discuss this question: How do you describe faith?

Key Verse

"Everything is possible for the person who has faith."

MARK 9:23 GNT

Video Lesson

Watch the session one video lesson now and fill in the blanks in the outline on pages 2 to 4. Refer back to the outline during your group discussion.

Lesson Outline

"Everything is possible for the person who has faith."

MARK 9:23 GNT

"According to your faith let it be done to you."

MATTHEW 9:29 NIV

Without faith it is impossible to please God.

HEBREWS 11:6 NIV

The Six Phases of Faith:

Phase 1: _____

Nothing happens in your life until you start dreaming.

How to Know If a Dream Is from God:

1. God's dream will always _____

God . . . is able to do far more than we would dare to ask or even dream of—infinitely beyond our highest prayers, desires, thoughts, or hopes.

EPHESIANS 3:20 TLB

If a dream comes from God, it's going to be so big, you can't do it on your own. You can only do it by faith.

Without faith it is impossible to please God.

HEBREWS 11:6 NIV

2. God's dream will never _____

Phase 2: _____

Nothing is going to happen to your dream until you wake up and put it in action.

The Decision Phase:

    1. You must _____ .

    2. You must _____ .

Phase 3: _____

There is always a waiting period between dream and fulfillment.

> *"These things I plan won't happen right away. Slowly, steadily, surely, the time approaches when the vision will be fulfilled. If it seems slow, do not despair, for these things will surely come to pass. Just be patient! They will not be overdue a single day!"*

> **HABAKKUK 2:3** TLB

God will not fulfill your dream immediately. Why? Because God wants to work on you before he works on the project.

Phase 4: _____

God uses difficulties to work on your faith and character.

> *At present you may be temporarily harassed by all kinds of trials. This is no accident—it happens to prove your faith, which is infinitely more valuable than gold.*

> **1 PETER 1:6-7** PHILLIPS

Phase 5: _____

Dead ends are a part of God's plan for your life.

> *At that time we were completely overwhelmed, the burden was more than we could bear, in fact we told ourselves that this was the end. Yet we believe now that we had this experience of coming to the end of our tether that we might learn to trust, not in ourselves, but in God who can raise the dead.*

> **2 CORINTHIANS 1:8-9** PHILLIPS

They said to Moses . . . "We told you to leave us alone and let us go on being slaves of the Egyptians. It would be better to be slaves there than to die here in the desert."

EXODUS 14:11–12 GNT

Dead ends are a part of God's plan for your life.

He has rescued us . . . and he will rescue us in the future. We are confident that he will continue to rescue us.

2 CORINTHIANS 1:10 GW

I am expecting the Lord to rescue me again, so that once again I will see his goodness to me.

PSALM 27:13 TLB

Phase 6: _____

The best response to a dead end is to expect God to act. What are you expecting God to do in your life?

Where God guides, God provides.

Great faith inspires great dreams.
Great dreams require great faith.

Living on Purpose

1. Which phase of faith are you currently in? Briefly explain your answer.

2. Of all the people you know personally, who do you believe has the strongest faith in God? Why is their faith so strong?

3. How does God's dream go beyond anything you could ever think up or imagine on your own?

4. When you understand the six phases of faith—dream, decision, delays, difficulties, dead ends, and deliverance—it prepares you for all that God wants to do in your future. Why is this so?

Prayer Direction

In what area of your life do you need your faith to be strengthened? Share your prayer requests, and then pray for each other. Use the Small Group Prayer and Praise Report beginning on page 95 to keep track of your requests.

Putting It into Practice

As you conclude this session, in what ways do you want God to help you grow spiritually and emotionally while you are pursuing his dream for your life?

God is faithful, and what he promises to do, he will do. Where God guides, God provides. But it doesn't happen overnight. You've got to go through all six phases of faith—dream, decision, delay, difficulty, and, finally, dead end—and then comes the deliverance.

Dreaming Is an
Act of Faith

DAY 1

God Holds
Everything Together

Did you know that God dreams? Just look around! Everything in the universe is something God dreamed up. You can't get past the first phrase of the first verse of the first chapter of the Bible without coming face-to-face with God's creativity. Genesis 1:1 says, *"In the beginning God created"* (NIV). God imagined and spoke everything into existence. It all began in God's mind. *"All things were made by him, and nothing was made without him. In him there was life, and that life was the light of all people"* (John 1:3–4 NCV).

If it weren't for God's loving control over all things, the world would stop spinning, and there would be no gravity. Everything would fall apart! Your life, your family—your whole existence—are held together by him. In fact, the Bible says, *"He existed before anything else, and he holds all creation together"* (Colossians 1:17 NLT).

1.   In what specific ways do you see God's creativity displayed all around you?

2. Even though you know God holds everything in the universe together, are there still things you have a hard time entrusting to God? What are those things?

Prayer: God, thank you that I can learn so much just by looking around me at all you have made. Help me to see with eyes of faith everything that reminds me that you are in control and care about every detail of my life.

DAY 2

God's Creativity on Display

We can learn a lot about God just by looking at nature. We see that he is powerful and that he loves beauty. We see that God cares about details and that he is organized. He has created all kinds of coordinated systems that interrelate—in the galaxies, in our environment, in your body, and in many other ways—and science continues to uncover new relationships between systems. He is a God of order and beauty.

Most of all, we see God's *creativity* in nature. Our Creator is extravagantly creative. Just think of all the plants and animals that fill the earth. He dreamed up every tree, every mountain, every planet—the whole universe! He dreamed up all the millions of variations in creatures and vegetation—and then he created you. He gave you the ability to create, too, by giving you the capacity to dream, imagine, and plan.

1. If God loves creativity and beauty and order and you are made in his image, what does that say about his dream for your life?

2. Do you think God wants you to apply your own creativity to the plans he has for you? Why or why not?

Prayer: *What a beautiful creation you have made, God! When I think about your dream for me, please show me how to apply the spirit of creativity and imagination that you gave me and have modeled for me.*

DAY 3

Your *God-Given* Ability

Before you took your first breath, God had already given you the gift of imagination. He hardwired creativity into every cell of your body. The Bible says that you were created in God's image (see Genesis 1:27). What does that mean?

You are a spiritual being. Your spirit is immortal and will outlast your earthly body.

You are intellectual. You can think, reason, and solve problems.

You are relational. You can give and receive love.

You have a moral consciousness. You can discern right from wrong, which makes you accountable to God.

You have the ability to dream. You can imagine doing something you have not yet experienced.

Your ability to dream of something you have not yet experienced is a God-given capacity that sets humans apart from the rest of creation. Fish can't imagine flying or even living out of water. Birds can't imagine living underwater. But humans have dreamed of both of these, and so much more, for ages.

What does all of this have to do with your spiritual development? Everything! Most people are unaware of the important connection between dreaming and faith. The truth is, men and women of deep faith have always been great dreamers.

We see examples throughout the Bible: Abraham, Joseph, Moses, Ruth, Esther, and many more. Instead of settling for the way things are in the world, people with strong faith imagine the possibilities of what *could* happen if they just trusted God a little bit more.

1. In what ways do you believe you have used your full potential for creativity? How have you seen someone else use their gifts for creativity in amazing ways?

2. If you knew your plans would not fail, what would you dream up for your life?

Prayer: *Father, I want to have the kind of faith that inspires great dreams for my life and encourages other believers to dream big in faith. Please strengthen my knowledge of you and my trust in you so that I expect you to do great things in my life.*

What Is Faith?

Faith stretches the imagination.
Faith risks failure.
Faith expects the best.
Faith waits for the answer.
Faith follows instructions.
Faith rebounds from setbacks.
Faith persists always.
Faith inspires great dreams.

Discovering *God's Dream* for You

Catching Up

Which stage of life are you in right now: Are you looking forward to a dream, are you living your dream, or have you given up on a dream?

Key Verse

My life is worth nothing to me unless I use it for finishing the work assigned me by the Lord Jesus.

ACTS 20:24 NLT

Video Lesson

Watch the session two video lesson now and fill in the blanks in the outline on pages 16 to 18. Refer back to the outline during your group discussion.

Lesson Outline

Nothing is more important, after coming to know Jesus Christ, than to get God's dream for your life.

> *"For I know the plans I have for you," declares the* Lord*, "plans to prosper you and not to harm you, plans to give you hope and a future."*
>
> **JEREMIAH 29:11** NIV

1. God's dream for you is _____ .
2. God's dream for you is _____ .

D _____ My Life to God

You've got to be willing to do whatever God wants you to do, even before he tells you to do it.

> *Offer yourselves as a living sacrifice to God, dedicated to his service. . . . Do not conform yourselves to the standards of this world, but let God transform you. . . . Then you will be able to know the will of God—what is good and is pleasing to him and is perfect.*
>
> **ROMANS 12:1–2** GNT

> *Do not conform yourselves to the standards of this world . . .*
>
> **ROMANS 12:2** GNT

> *Let us strip off anything that slows us down or holds us back . . . and let us run with patience the particular race that God has set before us.*
>
> **HEBREWS 12:1** TLB

> *My life is worth nothing to me unless I use it for finishing the work assigned me by the Lord Jesus.*
>
> **ACTS 20:24** NLT

R _____ **Time Alone with God**

You cannot get God's dream unless you spend time with God.

Pause a moment . . . and listen; consider the wonderful things God does.

JOB 37:14 GNT

God speaks to people who take time to listen.

E _____ **My Abilities**

Why would God give you certain gifts, and abilities, and talents—and then not use them?

For we are God's handiwork, created in Christ Jesus to devote ourselves to the good deeds for which God has designed us.

EPHESIANS 2:10 NEB

God has given each of you some special abilities; be sure to use them to help each other.

1 PETER 4:10 TLB

You are saved to serve. Use your talents and gifts to help other people.

Your young men shall see visions, your old men shall dream dreams.

ACTS 2:17 NKJV

A _____ **with Godly Dreamers**

Get around people who affirm God's dream rather than attack God's dream.

There's no such thing as a neutral friend. They're either pulling you toward God's dream or pulling you away from it.

As iron sharpens iron, so a friend sharpens a friend.

PROVERBS 27:17 NLT

Bad company corrupts good character.

1 CORINTHIANS 15:33 NIV

M _____ My Dream Public

Visualize the dream—and then verbalize the dream.

1. It gets _____ .

2. It attracts _____ .

3. It releases _____ .

The one who calls you is faithful, and he will do it.

1 THESSALONIANS 5:24 NIV

Nothing happens in your life until you start dreaming.

Living on Purpose

1. What do you believe God's dream is for your life?

2. Review the D.R.E.A.M. steps in the lesson outline. Which of these steps do you need to take?

3. What distractions do you need to eliminate today so that you can be still and quiet with God?

4. In what specific ways are you using your talents and gifts to serve others?

Prayer Direction

The dream phase of faith begins with dedicating all of yourself to God. In prayer, fully surrender your life to him. Invite him to be your Lord and ask him to open your eyes and give you his vision for your life. Pray for each other's requests.

Putting It into Practice

Pastor Rick said, "God speaks to people who take time to listen."

- If you currently practice a daily quiet time, over the next seven days, increase the amount of time you usually spend in devotions.

- If a quiet time with God is not part of your daily routine, over the next seven days, take ten minutes a day to review and pray about the Bible verses in this week's lesson outline.

God has a unique life course for you to run. It's your life mission, your dream, your purpose. If you're always looking at other people while you're running, you're going to end up trying to run their race, or you're going to get tripped up, or you're going to listen to people in the stands—and you'll miss out on God's race for you to run.

God's Custom-Made Dream for You

DAY 1

You Are *Unique*

God has a *"good, pleasing and perfect will"* (Romans 12:2 NIV) for your life. It's not a one-size-fits-all plan. God's dream for you is personal. It's custom-made for the way he shaped you.

In the session two video, I mentioned five important factors that make you, *you*. To help you remember them, I created a simple acrostic: SHAPE.

> **S**piritual gifts
> **H**eart
> **A**bilities
> **P**ersonality
> **E**xperiences

You are the only person in the world with your unique, God-given SHAPE. That means you are the only person who can fulfill God's dream for your life. Not only is God's dream personal; it is also positive. It's a plan *"to prosper you and not to harm you . . . to give you hope and a future"* (Jeremiah 29:11 NIV).

1. How does knowing your SHAPE help you decide if a dream you have is from God?

2. Read Romans 12:2. Why does conforming to the world's standards keep you from fulfilling the dream God has for you?

Prayer: Lord, I'm thankful for your good plan for me. Sometimes I don't feel motivated to take steps toward fulfilling my purpose. Please give me a sense of urgency about finding and following my dream so that I complete the work you made especially for me.

DAY 2

What Is *Your* SHAPE?

Here's a closer look at the five factors that influence your SHAPE:

Spiritual gifts are God-empowered abilities for serving him that are given only to believers. For instance, some gifts motivate you for ministry, like serving, teaching, encouraging, leading, giving, showing mercy, or offering biblical insight.

Heart refers to your bundle of desires, hopes, interests, ambitions, dreams, and affections. It's what you love to do and what you care about most. Have you ever noticed how deeply you feel about some things and not about other things? That's your heart.

Abilities are the natural talents you were born with. God wants you to do what he has enabled you to do. The Bible says, *"God has given us different gifts for doing certain things well"* (Romans 12:6 NLT).

Personality affects *how* and *where* you use your spiritual gifts and abilities. God has uniquely wired your temperament. He wants you to use your gifts in ways that are different from anybody else.

Experiences teach you lessons that help you mature. They also help you minister to others going through similar experiences.

 Take some time to think about and write down your SHAPE:

Spiritual gifts:

Heart:

Abilities:

Personality:

Experiences:

2. Think of a time you tried to pursue a dream or goal using abilities that did not fit your SHAPE. What was the result?

Prayer: *God, give me wisdom and help me discern the unique way you have shaped me so that I can give my whole life to pursuing your dream for me. Please show me through godly people the areas I cannot see that I need to grow in.*

DAY 3
Created for a Purpose

When God made you, he broke the mold. There is no one else like you! But, like most people, you may have never taken time to sort out and identify the things you're good at doing and motivated to accomplish. As a result, it is unlikely that you use these talents and abilities as completely and effectively as you could be using them.

One of the keys to understanding your SHAPE is to look at your past accomplishments. For example, what if you bought your first car at age sixteen, built a collection of rare stamps, and acquired three properties? It is clear that you are perfectly designed to acquire and collect meaningful things. Now you just need to ask God how he wants you to use your specific kind of motivation to fulfill his dream for your life.

Start praying today that you would find and follow God's dream for your life as you live and serve according to your SHAPE.

1. Write down a few of your accomplishments. What insight do they give you regarding the dream God created you to fulfill?

2. How can other people help you identify and apply your SHAPE? Is there someone in your life who can do that for you?

Prayer: *I'm ready to go after your dream for me, Lord! I need your help to be thoughtful about my SHAPE and your specific purpose for me. Thank you that you are always willing to lead me in the way I should go.*

Do You Want to Pursue God's Dream for Your Life?

Ask yourself: What am I good at doing? What gets me going in the morning? What energizes me and sets me in motion?

Ask others: What strengths do you see in me?

Ask God: How can you use this ability in your kingdom?

Making
Wise Decisions

Catching Up

How would you define wisdom?

Who is the wisest person you know?

Key Verse

If any of you need wisdom, you should ask God, and it will be given to you.

JAMES 1:5 CEV

Video Lesson

Watch the session three video lesson now and fill in the blanks in the outline on pages 30 to 32. Refer back to the outline during your group discussion.

Lesson Outline

A dream is worthless unless you wake up and act on it.

Life is not about making quick decisions. It's about making the *right* decisions.

God's Principles for Making Wise Decisions:

1. _____

Before you do anything else, get God's perspective on the issue.

> *If any of you need wisdom, you should ask God, and it will be given to you.*
>
> **JAMES 1:5** CEV

> *A man is foolish to trust himself! But those who use God's wisdom are safe.*
>
> **PROVERBS 28:26** TLB

Ask: _____ ?

2. _____

There is no contradiction between faith and fact. It's wise to find out all you can before you make a decision.

> *Every prudent man acts out of knowledge.*
>
> **PROVERBS 13:16** NCV

> *How stupid . . . to decide before knowing the facts!*
>
> **PROVERBS 18:13** TLB

Ask: _____ before I make this decision?

3. _____

> *The more good advice you get, the more likely you are to win.*
>
> **PROVERBS 24:6** GNT

It is wise to learn from experience, but it is wiser to learn from the experience of others.

We'd rather appear wise than *be* wise.

> *Get good advice and you will succeed.*
>
> **PROVERBS 20:18** GNT

Ask: _____ ?

4. _____

Every decision has a price tag.

> *It is a trap for a man to dedicate something rashly and only later to consider his vows.*
>
> **PROVERBS 20:25** NIV

Making a quick decision is not as important as making the right decision, and a right decision is an informed decision.

> *"Don't begin until you count the cost. For who would begin construction of a building without first calculating the cost to see if there is enough money to finish it? . . . Or what king would go to war against another king without first sitting down with his counselors to discuss whether his army of 10,000 could defeat the 20,000 soldiers marching against him?"*
>
> **LUKE 14:28, 31** NLT

Ask: _____ ?

5. _____

> *A sensible man watches for problems ahead and prepares to meet them. The simpleton never looks and suffers the consequences.*
>
> **PROVERBS 27:12** TLB

You can't ignore problems, because they are not going to ignore you. Prepare for problems, but don't try to solve all of them ahead of time.

Never confuse the decision-making phase with the problem-solving phase.

Ask: _____ ?

6. _____

Fear is at the root of all indecision.

> *Moses said . . ."They won't do what I tell them to. . . . I'm just not a good speaker."*
>
> **EXODUS 4:1, 10** TLB

> *Gideon replied . . . "I am the least in my family."*
>
> **JUDGES 6:15** NIV

> *Abraham . . . said to himself, "Will a son be born to a man a hundred years old?"*
>
> **GENESIS 17:17** NIV

> *If you wait for perfect conditions, you will never get anything done.*
>
> **ECCLESIASTES 11:4** TLB

Perfectionism paralyzes potential. The basic commitments of life must be made under imperfect conditions.

> *If God is for us, who can be against us?*
>
> **ROMANS 8:31** NIV

Ask: _____ ?

Not to decide is to decide. What decision do you need to make?

Living on Purpose

1. What decision are you facing that requires a step of faith?

2. Which of the six questions in the lesson outline is the most pressing for you right now? Explain.

3. At what point in the decision-making process do you usually ask God for his direction?

4. Why do you think God lets you decide how to live your life rather than making those decisions for you?

Prayer Direction

If you are in the decision phase, call on the Lord as your Counselor (see Isaiah 9:6). Ask him for wisdom and discernment and to help you make the right decision. Pray for each other's requests.

Putting It into Practice

What will you do between now and your next group meeting that will move you forward in the decision phase of faith?

Do something great with your life for Jesus' sake. Don't live a life of mediocrity. Don't drift through life. Don't just exist. Make the decision that you're going to follow hard after Christ. That will determine your destiny not just on earth, but also for all eternity.

Wake Up
and Act on It

DAY 1

The Most *Important* *Dream* of All

Did you ever dream about being famous? Maybe you dreamed about being the best in the world at something or the richest person you know.

Many of those dreams aren't worth your energy and time, because they are fleeting. That's why smart selection is key. You have to decide what dream is worth your life and what dream is not worth a second of your life.

There are actually three types of dreams. A dream can be the thoughts and images you have while sleeping. Not all those dreams are good; some are nightmares. Dreams can also be the passions and ambitions you have while you're awake, and they are more important than the dreams you have while sleeping. But the third type of dream, God's dream for your life, is the most important dream of all.

While you can dream up some amazing things, God's dream for you is personalized. As we discussed in session two, there's nobody else like you in the world. God gives you the ability to dream of new hobbies, new businesses, and new ministries, to dream about making a difference and changing your community, to dream of impacting the world. Pursuing God's unique dream for you is always the first step he uses in his process to change your life for the better. Everything starts as a dream.

1. What dream are you pursuing right now? What effects could it have for you and others?

2. How does knowing God's Word help you pursue God's dream?

Prayer: God, I have dreams for my life, but I want to pursue first the dream that you imagined for me even before I was born. Help me to trust that no matter how big the dreams are that I come up with on my own, your dream is always bigger and better.

DAY 2

No More *Excuses*

Children are naturally creative dreamers. They learn by playing "make-believe." As a child, you dreamed of doing things in your mind long before you actually did them. Yes, children are instinctively creative dreamers who imagine all kinds of things that adults know are "impossible."

But what happens to all that joyful creativity and dreaming? It gets crushed, stuffed, suppressed, stifled, and destroyed over time. It's tragic, but true. Typically, the older we get, the less we imagine and create. We procrastinate and avoid taking risks. And like Gideon who said, "I can't fight," Isaiah who said, "I'm too sinful," and Jeremiah who said, "I'm too young," we make excuses—and our dream becomes worthless, because we never wake up and act on it.

1. What are the most common distractions or obstructions to pursuing a dream or idea you have? What lies about yourself or your situation or even God keep you from going after big dreams?

2. Is there a dream you had when you were younger that seemed out of reach once you grew up? How can you apply what you now know about God to that big dream?

Prayer: *Lord, you know that I tend to procrastinate and make excuses, because I'm tired and frustrated. Please give me a renewed excitement for the plans you have for me and the discipline to follow through on them.*

DAY 3

Take a
Step of *Faith*

Nothing will happen to your dream until you wake up and put it into action. It all starts with the decision to go for it! For every ten dreamers in the world, there is only one decision maker. The only way to move forward in faith is to decide to take a risk.

Everything that humanity has accomplished in history started as a dream. Dreaming has always been an important part of being human. Since time began, people have taken great risks and dreamed great dreams. Whether it's launching a rocket into space or inventing self-driving cars, they imagined creating and doing things often years before those things became reality.

When you courageously imagine or dream of a better future for yourself, for your family, or for others, it's an act of faith. You're making the decision to believe that things *can* change and *can* be different, and you're believing that God will enable you to accomplish it. Faith is the key to achieving great things for God.

1.   In what ways has God already enabled you to accomplish your dream?

2. Beginning is often the hardest part of pursuing the dream you believe God has given you. But you don't have to take big steps toward your dream every day. How do you need to adjust your plans and expectations so you are more likely to take at least one small step every day in pursuit of your dream?

Prayer: When I look around me, God, it's easy to become discouraged and see things just as they are. Would you please give me your vision to see the potential in me, other people, and my situation so that I have the courage to take the next step of faith?

Bold Decision-Makers of the Bible

God gave **Noah** the dream of saving the world from the flood, but Noah had to make the decision to build the ark.

God gave **Abraham** the dream of being the father of a great nation, but Abraham had to make the decision to leave the comfort and security of home and step out into the unknown.

God gave **Moses** the dream of leading the children of Israel out of four hundred years of slavery, but Moses had to make the decision to confront Pharaoh.

Jesus called **the disciples** to join him in ministry, but they had to make the decision to walk away from their careers to follow him.

Jesus invited **Peter** to walk with him on the water, but Peter had to make the decision to get out of the boat and step into the miracle.

Persisting Through Delays

Catching Up

When is a specific time in your life when you experienced a delay in reaching a goal?

Key Verse

Let us not become tired of doing good; for if we do not give up, the time will come when we will reap the harvest.

GALATIANS 6:9 GNT

Video Lesson

Watch the session four video lesson now and fill in the blanks in the outline on pages 44 to 46. Refer back to the outline during your group discussion.

Lesson Outline

When Pharaoh finally let the people go, God did not lead them along . . . the shortest route to the Promised Land. God said, "If the people are faced with a battle, they might change their minds and return to Egypt."

EXODUS 13:17 NLT

God uses delays to _____ us.

God uses delays to _____ us.

The Lord led you through the wilderness for all those forty years . . . testing you to find out how you would respond, and whether or not you would really obey him."

DEUTERONOMY 8:2 TLB

When You're Going Through a Delay:

1. Don't _____

Fear keeps you in the wilderness and prolongs the delay.

> *The Lord said to Moses, "Send some men to explore the land of Canaan, which I am giving to the Israelites. . . . But the men who had gone up with him said, "We can't attack those people; they are stronger than we are."*

NUMBERS 13:1–2, 31 NIV

Fear keeps you stuck in the deserts of life.

> *"I will never leave you; I will never abandon you."*

HEBREWS 13:5 GNT

2. Don't _____

> *On the way the people lost their patience and spoke against God and Moses. They complained . . .*

NUMBERS 21:4–5 GNT

Rest in the Lord; wait patiently for him to act. . . . Don't fret and worry—it only leads to harm.

PSALM 37:7-8 TLB

Resting can be an act of faith. It means you're waiting on God.

3. Don't _____

All the Israelites grumbled against Moses . . . "If only we had died in Egypt! . . . We should choose a leader and go back to Egypt."

NUMBERS 14:2, 4 NIV

The Lord said to Joshua, "See, I have delivered Jericho into your hands. . . . The wall of the city will collapse and the army will go up."

JOSHUA 6:2, 5 NIV

"March around the city once with all the armed men. Do this for six days. . . . On the seventh day, march around the city seven times."

JOSHUA 6:3-4 NIV

Don't settle for less than God's best for your life. Instead of fainting, you need to be persistent and pray.

Let us never grow tired of doing what's right, for if we do not faint, we'll reap our harvest at the right time.

GALATIANS 6:9 MOFFATT

There is always a delay between sowing and reaping.

. . . always pray and never lose heart.

LUKE 18:1 PHILLIPS

They that wait upon the Lord shall renew their strength. They shall mount up with wings like eagles; they shall run and not be weary; they shall walk and not faint.

ISAIAH 40:31 TLB

4. Don't _____

They forgot the many times [God] showed them his love, and they rebelled against the Almighty at the Red Sea. But he saved them, as he had promised . . .

PSALM 106:7–8 GNT

But they soon forgot all he had done; they had no patience for his plan.

PSALM 106:13 NABRE

Has God done things for you in the past? Of course he has. And you can count on him to do them again.

I will bless the Lord and not forget the glorious things he does for me.

PSALM 103:2 TLB

The Lord is not being slow in carrying out his promises; rather, he is being patient with you.

2 PETER 3:9 NEW JERUSALEM BIBLE

A delay is not a denial . . . and "not yet" is not the same thing as "no."

These things I plan won't happen right away. Slowly, steadily, surely, the time approaches when the vision will be fulfilled. If it seems slow, do not despair, for these things will surely come to pass. Just be patient! They will not be overdue a single day!

HABAKKUK 2:3 TLB

There's always a delay between the dream and deliverance.

Living on Purpose

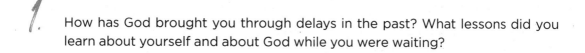

1. How has God brought you through delays in the past? What lessons did you learn about yourself and about God while you were waiting?

2. Review the Bible verses in the lesson outline. Which verse is the most meaningful to you at this time in your life? Why?

3. What is one thing you can change about your schedule or your expectations so that you are not tempted to try to rush God in the delay phase?

4. What do you need to change about your attitude as you spend time in God's waiting room?

Prayer Direction

If you are in the delay phase of faith, call on the Lord as your Sustainer (see Psalm 54:4). Ask him to give you patience and hope and to hold you up when you grow weary. Before you pray for each other's requests, take a few minutes to offer prayers of thanksgiving for God's blessings in your life.

Putting It into Practice

Remembering the things God has done in the past will build your faith as you face your current situation. Take ten minutes during a quiet time this week, and make a list that summarizes all the things God has done for you.

God is never in a hurry. We have no record in the New Testament that Jesus ever ran anywhere. God can do things immediately, and sometimes he does. But he is working on a much larger agenda than our timeframe. The delays that come into our lives do not destroy God's purposes. Rather, they fulfill God's purposes.

The Problem
of Worry

DAY 1
Fretting **Without** Fixing

I'm convinced there is a sign in God's waiting room that says, "Stop fretting, and start trusting." Aren't you glad God understands us? He knows our tendency to worry. He knows that when things take too long, we start stressing and griping—which is what the Israelites did.

Worry means you have forgotten God's goodness. Worry says, "God has dropped the ball. My problem is either too small for his attention or too big for him to handle. Either way, if it's to be, then it's up to me."

Worrying is also a waste of time. It's fretting without fixing. It's stewing without doing. Worrying is like sitting in a rocking chair: You expend a lot of energy, but you don't get anywhere. You just go back and forth, back and forth . . . should I or shouldn't I . . . will he or won't he . . . are they or aren't they . . . back and forth, back and forth, with absolutely no progress.

The only thing worry changes is you—it makes you miserable. The Bible says, *"Anxious hearts are very heavy"* (Proverbs 12:25 TLB), but, *"A relaxed attitude lengthens a man's life"* (Proverbs 14:30 TLB).

1. If worrying makes us miserable and takes a toll on our bodies, why do we so often do it as soon as we face trouble?

2. What problem have you been worrying about instead of bringing it to God because you thought it was not big enough for his attention? What can you do right now to bring it to God?

Prayer: *Father, please forgive me for how my lack of faith has caused me to worry, when I know that you are good all the time. Instead of worrying, I'm going to bring my concerns to you and then trust you with them.*

DAY 2

The Things *God Loves*

Worry can't make you one inch taller. Worry can't make you one inch shorter. Worry can't change the past, and it can't control the future. Worry will just mess up today.

So, instead of worrying, God says to fill your mind with *"whatsoever things are true, whatsoever things are honest, whatsoever things are just, whatsoever things are pure, whatsoever things are lovely, whatsoever things are of good report . . . and the God of peace shall be with you"* (Philippians 4:8–9 KJV).

You know you shouldn't worry, but does it ever seem like your mind has a mind of its own? You find yourself fretting over all the things that could go wrong rather than focusing on the "whatsoever" things, and you miss out on God's peace.

 How does God's Word help you to focus on the "whatsoever" things found in Philippians 4:8–9?

2. Even when it doesn't feel like it, you can still decide what you're going to think about. But it takes practice to set your mind on the things God loves. What is one practical thing you can do throughout your day for the next week that will help you refocus on things that are lovely and honest and just?

Prayer: I want to be so filled with faith in you, God, that there is no room for worry. Please give me a deeper love for your Word so that I grow in knowledge and truth and think more about the things you love.

DAY 3

A Renewed *Focus*

Typically, when we worry, it's because we've shifted our eyes off the Lord and onto the problem. We've taken our focus off the solution and put it on our circumstances.

Wouldn't you like to have a calm mind and a heart at rest? Turn your focus from your problem to God's power and purpose, reminding him of his promise: *"You will keep in perfect peace all who trust in you, all whose thoughts are fixed on you!"* (Isaiah 26:3 NLT).

In fact, the Bible says Jesus is the "Prince of Peace," because peace comes from his presence. If you turn away from Jesus, you won't experience the kind of peace that goes beyond all understanding (see Philippians 4:7) during the seasons you're stuck in God's waiting room.

Remember: God has a dream for your life. He put his Spirit in you when you placed your trust in Jesus. He will meet your needs. You don't need to worry.

1. Did you know that you can remind God of his promises? He loves when you remember what he has promised to do for you, and he wants you to tell him that you believe he will do it. What promise from the Bible do you need to claim today that will help you to not worry? If you can't think of one, you can start simply by doing a search online for God's promises.

2. Read Psalm 139:7–10. Where do you have to go to be in Jesus' presence?

Prayer: *Whenever I'm stuck on my problems (and it happens all the time), please turn my focus to you and all the things I know are true about you. Lord, thank you that you give me peace, even when I'm tired of waiting!*

Are You Persisting Through Delays?

Don't fear.

    Don't fret.

      Don't faint.

        Don't forget.

Be determined.

    Be diligent.

      Be disciplined.

        Be persisent.

          Be patient.

Dealing with
Difficulties

Catching Up

Complete this sentence: Life would be so much easier if . . .

Key Verse

We can rejoice, too, when we run into problems and trials, for we know . . . they help us learn to be patient.

ROMANS 5:3 TLB

Video Lesson

Watch the session five video lesson now and fill in the blanks in the outline on pages 58 to 60. Refer back to the outline during your group discussion.

Lesson Outline

"In this world you will have trouble. But take heart! I have overcome the world."

JOHN 16:33 NIV

In everything we do we show that we are God's servants by patiently enduring troubles, hardships, and difficulties.

2 CORINTHIANS 6:4 GNT

Paul warned them, "Men, I can see that our voyage is going to be disastrous and bring great loss to ship and cargo, and to our own lives also."

ACTS 27:9–10 NIV

Three Keys to Dealing with Difficulty:

1. Determine _____

Ask: What caused this?

> *I tried to think this problem through, but it was too difficult for me until I went into your Temple.*

PSALM 73:16–17 GNT

Three Common Mistakes:

1. We listen to _____ .

   The centurion, instead of listening to what Paul said, followed the advice of the pilot and of the owner of the ship.

ACTS 27:11 NIV

2. We follow _____ .

   The majority decided that we should sail . . .

ACTS 27:12 NIV

3. We rely on _____ .

   When a gentle south wind began to blow, they thought they had obtained what they wanted . . .

ACTS 27:13 NIV

2. Determine _____

Ask: What does God want me to learn?

We can rejoice, too, when we run into problems and trials, for we know . . . they help us learn to be patient. And patience develops strength of character in us and helps us trust God more each time . . .

ROMANS 5:3–4 TLB

Every problem has a purpose.

He doesn't want you to give up; he wants you to grow up.

3. Determine _____

Ask: How should I react?

What happens _____ you is not as important as what happens _____ you.

Three Wrong Responses to Difficulty:

1. Don't _____

The ship was caught by the storm and could not head into the wind; so we gave way to it and were driven along.

ACTS 27:15 NIV

2. Don't _____

They began to throw the cargo overboard.

ACTS 27:18 NIV

Paul said to the centurion and the soldiers, "Unless these men stay with the ship, you cannot be saved." So the soldiers cut the ropes that held the lifeboat and let it drift away.

ACTS 27:31–32 NIV

3. Don't _____

We finally gave up all hope of being saved.

ACTS 27:20 NIV

Three Right Responses to Difficulty:

1. _____

What are you pretending is not a problem?

> *A man who refuses to admit his mistakes can never be successful. But if he confesses and forsakes them, he gets another chance.*

PROVERBS 28:13 TLB

2. _____

The only way to face a storm is head-on. Face the storm. Don't fear it.

3. _____

Everything was falling apart in the storm except Paul. Why? Because Paul's confidence was in God, not in the ship.

> *"Keep up your courage, men, for I have faith in God that it will happen just as he told me."*

ACTS 27:25 NIV

You may be going through a storm right now, and your ship may not make it. But *you* will make it.

You may have to get to shore on a broken piece of the ship, but you will not be lost, because God is with you. Don't give up.

Living on Purpose

1. Pastor Rick said, "Every problem has a purpose, and the purpose is to teach you a lesson. What happens *to* you is not as important as what happens *in* you." What do you think God is trying to teach you through the difficulties you are facing right now, and how does he want you to respond?

2. When did you run from a difficult situation? When did you stay in a difficult situation? How did your response in each situation shape your character?

3. What outcome from your difficulty do you believe will bring the most glory to God?

4. What kind of trouble have you encountered because of a mistake you made in responding to a difficulty? How did God deliver you in that situation?

Prayer Direction

If you are in the difficulty phase of faith, call on the Lord as your Shield (see Psalm 28:7). Ask him to give you strength and courage and to protect you from Satan. Pray for anyone in your group who is going through a storm right now.

Putting It into Practice

Take a few minutes this week to review each step in the outline from Pastor Rick's lesson, and ask yourself, "How does this step apply to the difficulty I'm facing?"

Don't start drifting through life. Don't throw away those values and relationships that you know are important. Don't throw away your relationship with God, or going to church, or being a part of your small group, or reading your Bible. Don't drift. Don't discard. Don't despair. Instead, turn to God and never give up hope.

God's Long-Range
Plans for You

DAY 1

Dreaming **with** *Purpose*

Your dreams profoundly shape your identity, your happiness, your achievements, and your fulfillment. But the benefits of God-inspired dreaming are far more important than just these; God's dream has *eternal* implications, too.

There are many things you will have to endure in life. You'll struggle through mistakes, sins, embarrassments, and failures. But remember: what happens to you is not nearly as important as what happens in you. Why? Because what happens to you is tempo-rary, but what happens in you is eternal. God is far more interested in the person you are becoming than in your accomplishments. Why? Because you're not taking your accomplishments to heaven—but you are taking *you*.

The deeper purpose of your God-given dream is what you become as you go after that dream. Romans 5:3-4 says, *"We can rejoice, too, when we run into problems and trials, for we know that they help us develop endurance. And endurance develops strength of character"* (NLT).

The process God uses to move you toward spiritual and emotional maturity begins with dreaming. It is the catalyst for personal change, but dreaming is just the first phase. As we've been learning in this study, there are five more phases—decision, delays, difficulties, dead ends, and deliverance—that God will take us through over and over to prepare us for life with him in heaven.

1. Why do you think God develops your spiritual maturity over time and doesn't just produce it in you instantly when you become a Christian?

2. Where do you get the patience to endure when you know that there are more steps to your dream ahead of you, especially when you are still in the difficulty phase?

Prayer: God, it's hard for me to imagine being the kind of person who can rejoice in my suffering and problems, but that's who I want you to help me become. I'm so thankful that you have promised to finish the work you are doing in me, no matter how I mess up.

DAY 2

Keeping *Eternity* in Mind

You may be more interested in reaching your dream on earth, but God is more interested in building your character for heaven. Why? Because God has long-range plans for you that will far outlast your brief time on earth. God has a longer view of you. He's looking at your life in light of eternity.

Any goal or dream that you envision happening here on earth will be short-term, because everything on earth is temporary. We're just passing through. This is just the warm-up act before real life begins on the other side of death. Life on earth doesn't last. But life in eternity will last forever.

1. Spend some time thanking God that there is more to life and eternity than what you can see and envision. Thank him and praise him for planning a dream for your life that will last forever and is always good.

2. How can you keep eternity in mind when you are pursuing your dream?

Prayer: Lord, please give me an eternal perspective on everything I am enduring right now. Help me to see better how you are working in me and producing spiritual fruit in me that would not have happened any other way.

DAY 3

The Person
You're Becoming

When you die, you're not going to take your career to heaven. You're not going to take your clothes or your cars or your cash either. You'll leave everything behind. The only thing you'll take into eternity is *you*! That means the only thing of yours that will last is your character and the person you chose to become.

The Bible is blunt: *"For we brought nothing into the world, and we can take nothing out of it"* (1 Timothy 6:7 NIV). That's why God considers what *you become* on earth far more important than what you do while you're here. So, while you're working on your dream, God will be working on your character.

Here's the good news: God promises that if you cooperate with him, then he will complete the makeover in your heart. The Bible says, *"I am certain that God, who began the good work within you, will continue his work until it is finally finished on that day when Christ Jesus returns"* (Philippians 1:6 NLT).

1.   Are you pursuing God's dream for you over your career or your material goals? In what ways?

2. How can Philippians 1:6 encourage you as you walk through the difficulty phase of your dream? What steps can you take this week to start committing this verse to memory?

Prayer: *I want to cooperate with you in the work you are doing in my life, God. I will look to you so that I can work confidently on my dream because I know that you are always working on me.*

Every Problem
Has a Purpose

Every storm is a school.

Every trial is a teacher.

Every experience is an education.

Every difficulty is for your development.

From *Dead Ends* to *Deliverance*

Catching Up

Does anyone have an update about an answer to your group's prayers for them?

Does anything feel impossible in your life right now?

Key Verse

"What is impossible with men is possible with God."

LUKE 18:27 NIV

Video Lesson

Watch the session six video lesson now and fill in the blanks in the outline on pages 72 to 74. Refer back to the outline during your group discussion.

Lesson Outline

Faith is the substance of things hoped for, the evidence of things not seen.

HEBREWS 11:1 NKJV

God said, "Take your son . . . and go to the region of Moriah. Sacrifice him there as a burnt offering."

GENESIS 22:2 NIV

While You're Waiting for God's Deliverance:

1. _____ what God can do

The situation may be out of your control, but it's not out of God's control.

> *Abraham believed [in] God who gives life to the dead and who creates something out of nothing.*
>
> **ROMANS 4:17** NCV

When you face things that are out of your control, you need more than a positive mental attitude. You need faith in God.

> *"What is impossible with men is possible with God."*
>
> **LUKE 18:27** NIV

2. _____ on what God has said

> *When hope was dead within him, [Abraham] went on hoping in faith. . . . He relied on the word of God.*
>
> **ROMANS 4:18** PHILLIPS

How do you know when hope is dead? You start using the word "never."

> *While God was testing him, Abraham still trusted in God and his promises, and so he offered up his son Isaac.*
>
> **HEBREWS 11:17** TLB

Isaac spoke up and said to his father . . . "Where is the lamb for the burnt offer-ing?" Abraham answered, "God himself will provide."

GENESIS 22:7–8 NIV

3. _____ with faith

Without weakening in his faith, he faced the fact that his body was as good as dead . . . and that Sarah's womb was also dead. Yet he did not waver through unbelief.

ROMANS 4:19–20 NIV

Faith is not denying reality. Faith is facing the facts without being discouraged by them.

We fix our eyes not on what is seen, but on what is unseen, since what is seen is temporary, but what is unseen is eternal.

2 CORINTHIANS 4:18 NIV

Let us fix our eyes on Jesus, the author and perfecter of our faith.

HEBREWS 12:2 NIV

4. _____ God to deliver me

What are you expecting God to do? God works in your life according to your expectations.

"According to your faith let it be done to you."

MATTHEW 9:29 NIV

Abraham never doubted. . . . He praised God for this blessing even before it happened. He was completely sure that God was well able to do anything he promised.

ROMANS 4:20–21 TLB

The ultimate form of faith is thanking God in advance for what he is going to do. Abraham praised God for the blessing, even before it happened.

> But this happened that we might not rely on ourselves but on God, who raises the dead. He has delivered us . . . he will deliver us. . . . We have set our hope that he will continue to deliver us.
>
> 2 CORINTHIANS 1:9–10 NIV

Three Kinds of Deliverance:

1. _____ (or *external*) deliverance.

2. _____ (or *internal*) deliverance.

3. _____ (or *eternal*) deliverance (heaven).

The world hopes for the best, but Jesus is your best hope.

Jesus is our Savior, which means Jesus is our Deliverer.

> Jesus answered, "I am the way and the truth and the life. No one comes to the Father except through me."
>
> JOHN 14:6 NIV

Jesus can take a hopeless end and turn it into an endless hope.

If you are saved, it means that you are already delivered.
Your ultimate delivery is going to be an eternity in heaven.

Living on Purpose

1. What life experiences came to mind as you listened to Pastor Rick's message? Does anyone have a story to share of a time when God delivered you from a dead end?

2. How does remembering who God is and what he can do help you as you wait for his deliverance?

3. What promises from God encourage you when you are at a dead end?

4. What is the most meaningful lesson you have learned in this study? What step will you take today to start to apply that lesson in your life?

Prayer Direction

If you are in the dead-end phase of faith, call on the Lord as your Deliverer (see Psalm 18:2). Ask him to restore your hope and trust in him and to make a way where there is no way. Before you pray for each other's requests, thank God for the lessons in faith that he has taught you through this study.

Putting It into Practice

Your story of faith can change someone else's life. Who do you know who needs to hear about the six phases of faith? Make a plan to share with them the faith-building lessons you have learned through this study.

The ultimate form of faith is thanking God in advance for what you are presently asking him to do. If you thank him after he has answered your prayer, that is not faith but gratitude. When you're at a dead end, choose to thank God that the answer is already on the way.

The Key to
Deliverance

DAY 1

Thanking God in Advance

The key to deliverance is faith-filled gratitude. When you're at a dead end, and it seems like your dream will never come to pass, thank God that your deliverance is already on its way, even if you don't see it yet. Thanking God in advance is a big step of faith—and God always responds to faith!

Maybe you're at a dead end today, and you don't feel like thanking God in advance. You've been waiting on God for a miracle—a release from a hurt, an answer to a prayer, a breakthrough in an otherwise impossible situation—and you are losing hope that God's dream will come true.

Or maybe God has given you a specific promise that's not ending the way you believed it would or according to what you know to be true in Scripture. You've held on to it for a long time, and now you're tempted to let go.

You need to remember that God is not limited by your time on earth to fulfill his promises. Jesus said, *"Heaven and earth will pass away, but my words will never pass away"* (Matthew 24:35 NIV). You can still hold on to the truth without insisting that the promise be fulfilled on your timetable. God has all of eternity to keep his word!

1. What can you thank God for in advance when it comes to the specific dream he's given you?

2. Would you be satisfied and trust God if you knew that he was going to fulfill your dream in eternity and not here on earth? Why or why not?

Prayer: *Even when I'm facing what looks like a dead end in my dream, Lord, you have not changed, and you have not stopped working. I believe in your promise to deliver me, and I thank you for how you are making me more like you in the process.*

DAY 2

The God of
Second Chances

Start thanking God right now for the deliverance that is already on its way. Jesus can take that hopeless end and turn it into an endless hope. Even if you face many dead ends, God will deliver you over and over again on earth and then ultimately in heaven one day. Why? Because the *"steadfast love of the LORD never ceases; his mercies never come to an end; they are new every morning"* (Lamentations 3:22–23 ESV).

You see, God is a God of second chances. God is a God who does new things. He doesn't do the same old things all the time. He'll often give you multiple dreams throughout your lifetime. God says in Isaiah 43:18–19, *"Do not cling to events of the past or dwell on what happened long ago. Watch for the new thing I am going to do. It is happening already—you can see it now!"* (GNT).

So trust him. Hold on to him. And remember, *"God can do anything, you know—far more than you could ever imagine or guess or request in your wildest dreams! He does it not by pushing us around but by working within us, his Spirit deeply and gently within us"* (Ephesians 3:20 MSG).

1. How can you show God that you believe your deliverance is already on its way?

2. When you feel like you're being pushed around in the pursuit of your dream, remember that God does not play games with you. He is always good and always generous with his grace. How have you already seen his Spirit working in you?

Prayer: God, it's awesome to know that you do not give up on me and you are always doing something new in my life. Help me not to give up on my dream, because I believe that you will provide for me until it is completed.

DAY 3

God Is *Faithful*

The dream God created you to fulfill has been on his mind since he formed you in your mother's womb. What he calls you to do, he will enable you to do—in his timing and in his way. You don't have any right to complain, gripe, argue, or doubt, because he's going to do what he said he would do. God is faithful. But he will take you through these six phases of faith, from the dream to decision to delays to difficulties to dead ends and to deliverance. They are not a one-time experience; he will take you through them many times. In Psalm 50:15, God says, "*I want you to trust me in your times of trouble, so I can rescue you and you can give me glory*" (TLB).

When you persist in your dream, believing God will fulfill his promises to you, then you will give him glory.

1. When has God taken you through the six phases of faith before? What did you learn about God through that process? In what ways did you become more like Jesus?

2. Who are the people who will help you persist in the pursuit of God's dream for your life?

Prayer: Lord, as I go through the six phases of faith, I'm trusting you to fulfill every promise and do every good work in me and deliver me so that I can bring you glory. I praise you in whatever phase I am in today and ask you to help me persist in going after the dream you created me to dream.

Ten Truths About Dreams

1. Dreams show what God wants to do through you.
2. Dreams define you.
3. Dreams keep you growing.
4. Dreams clarify your priorities.
5. Dreams build your character.
6. Dreams deepen your courage.
7. Dreams stretch your faith.
8. Dreams inspire others to dream.
9. Dreams focus your energy.
10. Dreams reveal God's glory.

Top Ten Ideas for Helping Your Group Succeed

Congratulations! As the host of your small group, you have committed to help shepherd Jesus' flock. Few other tasks in God's family surpass the contribution you will be making. As you prepare to facilitate this study in your group, here are a few thoughts to keep in mind.

Remember you are not alone. God knows everything about you, and he knew you would be asked to host your group. Even though you may not feel ready, this is common for all good hosts. God promises, *"I will never leave you; I will never abandon you"* (Hebrews 13:5 GNT). Whether you are facilitating for one evening, several weeks, or a lifetime, you will be blessed as you serve.

1. Don't try to do it alone. Pray right now for God to help you build a healthy team. If you can enlist a cohost to help you shepherd the group, you will find your experience much richer. This is your chance to involve as many people as you can in building a healthy group. All you have to do is ask people to help. You'll be surprised at the response!

2. Be friendly and be yourself. God wants to use your unique gifts and personality. Be sure to greet people at the door with a smile; this can set the mood for the whole gathering. Remember, they are taking as big a step as you are to show up at your house! Don't try to do things exactly like another host. Do them in a way that fits you. Admit when you don't have an answer and apologize when you make a mistake. Your group will love you for it, and you'll sleep better at night.

3. Prepare for your meeting ahead of time. Review the session and write down your responses to each question. Pay special attention to the Putting It into Practice exercises that ask group members to do something other than engage in discussion. These exercises will help your group live what the Bible teaches, not just talk about it.

4. Pray for your group members by name. Before you begin your session, take a few moments and pray for each member by name. You will want to review the prayer list at least once a week. Ask God to use your time together to touch the heart of every person in your group. Expect God to lead you to whomever he wants you to encourage or challenge in a special way. If you listen, God will surely lead.

5. When you ask a question, be patient. Someone will eventually respond. Sometimes people need a moment or two of silence to think about the question. If silence doesn't bother you, it won't bother anyone else. After someone responds, affirm the response with a simple "Thanks." Then ask, "How about somebody else?" or "Would someone who hasn't shared like to add anything?" Be sensitive to new people or reluctant members who aren't ready to speak, pray, or do anything. If you give them a safe setting, they will blossom over time. If someone in your group is a wallflower who sits silently through every session, consider talking to them privately and encouraging them to participate. Let them know how important they are to you, that they are loved and appreciated, and the group values their input. Remember, still water often runs deep.

6. Provide transitions between questions. Ask if anyone would like to read the paragraph or Bible passage. Don't call on anyone, but ask for a volunteer, and then be patient until someone begins. Be sure to thank the person who reads aloud.

7. Break into smaller groups occasionally. With a greater opportunity to talk in a small circle, people will connect more with the study, apply more quickly what they're learning, and ultimately get more out of their small group experience. A small circle also encourages a quiet person to participate and tends to minimize the effects of a more vocal or dominant member.

8. Small circles are also helpful during prayer time. People who are unaccustomed to praying aloud will feel more comfortable trying it with just two or three others. Also, prayer requests won't take as much time, so circles will have more time to actually pray. When you gather back with the whole group, you can have one person from each circle briefly update everyone on the prayer requests from their smaller groups.

These smaller groups also foster leadership development. As you ask people in the group to facilitate discussion or to lead a prayer circle, it gives them a small leadership step that can build their confidence.

9. Rotate facilitators occasionally. You may be perfectly capable of hosting each time, but you will help others grow in their faith and gifts if you give them opportunities to host the group.

10. One final challenge (for new or first-time hosts). Before your first opportunity to lead, look up each of the six passages that follow. Read each one as a devotional exercise to help prepare you with a shepherd's heart. If you do this, you will be more than ready for your first meeting.

When [Jesus] saw the crowds, he had compassion on them, because they were harassed and helpless, like sheep without a shepherd. Then he said to his disciples, "The harvest is plentiful but the workers are few. Ask the Lord of the harvest, therefore, to send out workers into his harvest field."

MATTHEW 9:36–38 NIV

"I am the good shepherd; I know my sheep and my sheep know me—just as the Father knows me and I know the Father—and I lay down my life for the sheep."

JOHN 10:14–15 NIV

Be shepherds of God's flock that is under your care, watching over them—not because you must, but because you are willing, as God wants you to be; not pursuing dishonest gain, but eager to serve; not lording it over those entrusted to you, but being examples to the flock. And when the Chief Shepherd appears, you will receive the crown of glory that will never fade away.

1 PETER 5:2–4 NIV

If you have any encouragement from being united with Christ, if any comfort from his love, if any common sharing in the Spirit, if any tenderness and compassion, then make my joy complete by being like-minded, having the same love, being one in spirit and of one mind. Do nothing out of selfish ambition or vain conceit. Rather, in humility value others above yourselves, not looking to your own interests but each of you to the interests of the others. In your relationships with one another, have the same mindset as Christ Jesus.

PHILIPPIANS 2:1–5 NIV

Let us hold unswervingly to the hope we profess, for he who promised is faithful. And let us consider how we may spur one another on toward love and good deeds, not giving up meeting together, as some are in the habit of doing, but encouraging one another—and all the more as you see the Day approaching.

HEBREWS 10:23–25 NIV

Instead, we were like young children among you. Just like a nursing mother cares for her children, so we cared for you. Because we loved you so much, we were delighted to share with you not only the gospel of God but our lives as well. . . . For you know that we dealt with each of you as a father deals with his own children, encouraging, comforting and urging you to live lives worthy of God, who calls you into his kingdom and glory.

1 THESSALONIANS 2:7–8, 11–12 NIV

Frequently Asked Questions

How long will this group meet?

This study is six sessions long. We encourage your group to add a seventh session for a celebration. In your final session, each group member may decide if they desire to continue on for another study. At that time, you may also want to do some informal evaluation, discuss your group guidelines, and decide which study you want to do next. We recommend you visit pastors.com for more video-based small group studies.

Who is the host?

The host is the person who coordinates and facilitates your group meetings. In addition to a host, we encourage you to select one or more group members to lead your group discussions. Several other responsibilities can be rotated, including refreshments, prayer requests, worship, or keeping up with those who miss a meeting. Shared ownership in the group helps everybody grow.

Where do we find new group members?

Recruiting new members can be a challenge for groups, especially new groups with just a few people or existing groups that lose a few people along the way. We encourage you to use the Circles of Life diagram on page 93 of this study guide to brainstorm a list of people from your workplace, church, school, neighborhood, family, and so on. Then pray for the people on each member's list. Allow each member to invite several people from their list.

Some groups fear that newcomers will interrupt the intimacy that members have built over time. However, groups that welcome newcomers generally gain strength with the addition of fresh perspectives. Remember, the next person you add just might become a friend for eternity. Logistically, groups find different ways to add members. Some groups remain permanently open, while others choose to open periodically, such as at the beginning or end of a study. If your group becomes too large for easy, face-to-face conversations, you can subgroup, forming a second discussion group in another room.

How do we handle the childcare needs in our group?

Childcare needs must be handled very carefully. This is a sensitive issue. We suggest you seek creative solutions as a group. One common solution is to have the adults meet in the living room and share the cost of a babysitter (or two) who can be with the kids in another part of the house. Another popular option is to have one home for the kids and a second home (close by) for the adults. If desired, the adults could rotate the responsibility of providing a lesson for the kids. This last option is great with school-age kids and can be a huge blessing to families.

Group Guidelines

It's a good idea for every group to put words to their shared values, expectations, and commitments. Such guidelines will help you avoid unspoken agendas and unmet expectations. We recommend you discuss your guidelines during session one in order to lay the foundation for a healthy group experience. Feel free to modify anything that does not work for your group.

We agree to the following values:	
Clear Purpose	To grow healthy spiritual lives by building a healthy small group community
Group Attendance	To give priority to the group meeting (call if we are absent or late)
Safe Environment	To create a safe place where people can be heard and feel loved (no quick answers, snap judgments, or simple fixes)
Be Confidential	To keep anything that is shared strictly confidential and within the group
Conflict Resolution	To avoid gossip and to immediately resolve any concerns by following the principles of Matthew 18:15–17
Spiritual Health	To give group members permission to speak into our lives and help us live healthy, balanced spiritual lives that are pleasing to God
Limit Our Freedom	To limit our freedom by not serving or consuming alcohol during small group meetings or events so as to avoid causing a weaker brother or sister to stumble (see 1 Corinthians 8:1–13; Romans 14:19–21)

We agree to the following values:	
Welcome Newcomers	To invite friends who might benefit from this study and warmly welcome newcomers
Building Relationships	To get to know the other members of the group and pray for them regularly
Other	

We have also discussed and agree on the following items:

Childcare _____

Starting Time _____

Ending Time _____

If you haven't already done so, take a few minutes to fill out the Small Group Calendar on page 94.

Circles of Life

Discover Who You Can Connect in Community

Use this chart to help carry out one of the values in the Group Guidelines, to "Welcome Newcomers."

"Follow me, and I will show you how to fish for people!"

MATTHEW 4:19 NLT

Follow this simple three-step process:

1. List one or two people in each of the circles in the chart below.
2. Prayerfully select one person or family from your list and tell your group about them.
3. Give that person or family a call and invite them to your next meeting. More than fifty percent of those invited to a small group say yes!

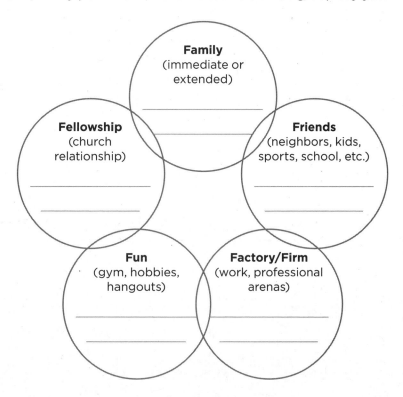

Small Group Calendar

Healthy groups share responsibilities and group ownership. It might take some time for this to develop. Shared ownership ensures that responsibility for the group doesn't fall to one person. Use the calendar to keep track of social events, mission projects, birthdays, or days off. Complete this calendar at your first or second meeting. Planning ahead will increase attendance and shared ownership.

Date	Session	Location	Facilitator	Snack/Meal
	Session 1			
	Session 2			
	Session 3			
	Session 4			
	Session 5			
	Session 6			
	Celebration			

Small Group Prayer and Praise Report

This is a place where you can write each other's requests for prayer. You can also make a note when God answers a prayer. Pray for each other's requests. If you're new to group prayer, it's okay to pray silently or to pray by using just one sentence: "God, please help _____ to _____."

Date	Person	Prayer Request	Praise/Update

Answer Key

Session 1: How Faith and Dreaming Are Connected
The Six Phases of Faith:

Phase 1: <u>Dream</u>
> 1. God's dream will always require faith
> 2. God's dream will never contradict God's Word

Phase 2: <u>Decision</u>
> 1. You must <u>invest</u>
> 2. You must <u>let go of security</u>

Phase 3: <u>Delay</u>

Phase 4: <u>Difficulty</u>

Phase 5: <u>Dead End</u>

Phase 6: <u>Deliverance</u>

Session 2: Discovering God's Dream for You
> 1. God's dream for you is <u>personal</u>
> 2. God's dream for you is <u>postive</u>

<u>Dedicate</u> My Life to God

<u>Reserve</u> Time Alone with God

<u>Evaluate</u> My Abilities

<u>Associate</u> with Godly Dreamers

<u>Make</u> My Dream Public
> 1. It gets <u>you started</u>
> 2. It attracts <u>other people</u>
> 3. It releases <u>God's power</u>

Session 3: Making Wise Decisions
God's Principles for Making Wise Decisions:

> 1. <u>Pray for guidance</u>
>   Ask: <u>What does God want?</u>
> 2. <u>Get the facts</u>
>   Ask: <u>What do I need to know</u> before I make this decision?
> 3. <u>Ask for advice</u>
>   Ask: <u>Who can I talk to?</u>

4. Calculate the cost
   Ask: Is it worth it?
5. Prepare for problems
   Ask: What could go wrong?
6. Face your fears
   Ask: What am I afraid of?

Session 4: Persisting Through Delays

God uses delays to prepare us.

God uses delays to test us.

When You're Going Through a Delay:

1. Don't fear
2. Don't fret
3. Don't faint
4. Don't forget

Session 5: Dealing with Difficulties

Three Keys to Dealing with Difficulty:

1. Determine the reason

   Three Common Mistakes:

   1. We listen to bad advice.
   2. We follow the crowd.
   3. We rely on circumstances.

2. Determine the result
3. Determine your response

   What happens to you is not as important as what happens in you.

Three Wrong Responses to Difficulty:

1. Don't drift
2. Don't discard
3. Don't despair

Three Right Responses to Difficulty:

1. Confess my part
2. Confront it
3. Claim a promise

Session 6: From Dead Ends to Deliverance

While You're Waiting for God's Deliverance:

1. Remember what God can do

2. <u>Rely</u> on what God has said

3. <u>Face the facts</u> with faith

4. <u>Expect</u> God to deliver me

Three Kinds of Deliverance:

1. <u>Circumstantial</u> (or *external*) deliverance

2. <u>Personal</u> (or *internal*) deliverance

3. <u>Ultimate</u> (or *eternal*) deliverance (heaven)

Key Verses

One of the most effective ways to support the principles we are learning in this series is to memorize key passages of Scripture. For many, memorization is a new concept or one that has been difficult in the past. We encourage you to stretch yourself and try to memorize the key verses for this study. If possible, memorize them as a group, and make them part of your group time. You may cut these apart and carry them in your wallet.

Session 1: How Faith and Dreaming Are Connected

"Everything is possible for the person who has faith."

MARK 9:23 GNT

Session 2: Discovering God's Dream for You

My life is worth nothing to me unless I use it for finishing the work assigned me by the Lord Jesus.

ACTS 20:24 NLT

Session 3: Making Wise Decisions

If any of you need wisdom, you should ask God, and it will be given to you.

JAMES 1:5 CEV

Session 4: Persisting Through Delays

Let us not become tired of doing good; for if we do not give up, the time will come when we will reap the harvest.

GALATIANS 6:9 GNT

Session 5: Dealing with Difficulties

We can rejoice, too, when we run into problems and trials, for we know . . . they help us learn to be patient.

ROMANS 5:3 TLB

Session 6: From Dead Ends to Deliverance

"What is impossible with man is possible with God."

LUKE 18:27 NIV

About the Author

A *Time* magazine cover article named Rick Warren the most influential spiritual leader in America and one of the 100 most influential people in the world.

Tens of millions of copies of Pastor Rick's books have been published in 200 languages. His best-known books, *The Purpose Driven Life* and *The Purpose Driven Church*, were named three times in national surveys of pastors (by Gallup, Barna, and Lifeway) as the two most helpful books in print.

Rick and his wife, Kay, founded Saddleback Church, the Purpose Driven Network, the PEACE Plan, and Hope for Mental Health. He is the cofounder of Celebrate Recovery with John Baker.

Pastor Rick has spoken in 165 nations. He has spoken at the United Nations, US Congress, numerous parliaments, the World Economic Forum, TED, Aspen Institute, and lectured at Oxford, Cambridge, Harvard, and other universities.

Rick is executive director of Finishing the Task, a global movement of denominations, organizations, churches, and individuals working together on the Great Commission goals of ensuring that everyone everywhere has access to a Bible, a believer, and a local body of Christ.

One Last Thing . . .

I'm so glad you're taking steps to discover and follow God's dream for your life.

I've often thought that extraordinary people are just ordinary people who attach themselves to an extraordinary dream—God's dream. And I'm convinced that nothing else in life will provide a greater sense of fulfillment than doing what God made you to do.

To encourage you as you move toward all God has for you, I created Daily Hope—my FREE email devotional and podcast that delivers Bible teaching to your inbox every day. Connecting to Daily Hope will inspire you to study God's Word and build a deep, meaningful relationship with him, which is essential to living the life you were meant to live.

I'm excited to help guide you on your journey, because pursuing God's dream is the greatest adventure you will ever experience.

Pastor Rick

Take the Next Step . . .
Get my FREE Daily Hope devotional at **PastorRick.com/Dream**